Pet Care

Goldfish

Kelley MacAulay & Bobbie Kalman

Photographs by Marc Crabtree

Illustrations by Margaret Amy Reiach

🌳 Crabtree Publishing Company

www.crabtreebooks.com

Goldfish

A Bobbie Kalman Book

Dedicated by Mike Golka
To my little fry, Amber & Russell

Editor-in-Chief
Bobbie Kalman

Writing team
Kelley MacAulay
Bobbie Kalman

Editors
Molly Aloian
Amanda Bishop
Kristina Lundblad
Kathryn Smithyman

Art director
Robert MacGregor

Design
Margaret Amy Reiach

Production coordinator
Katherine Kantor

Photo research
Crystal Foxton

Consultant
Dr. Michael A. Dutton, DVM, DABVP
Exotic and Bird Clinic of New Hampshire
www.ExoticAndBirdClinic.com

Special thanks to
Keith Makubuya, Sarah Chan, Lori Chan, Zachary
Murphy, Candice Murphy, Mike Cipryk, and PETLAND

Photographs
Marc Crabtree: front cover, title page, pages 3, 5, 6, 7,
    14, 16-17, 18, 19, 20, 21, 22, 23, 24, 25, 26, 27, 30-31
Robert MacGregor: pages 12 (except goldfish), 13
Other images by PhotoDisc

Illustrations
All illustrations by Margaret Amy Reiach

Crabtree Publishing Company

www.crabtreebooks.com   1-800-387-7650

Copyright © **2005 CRABTREE PUBLISHING COMPANY.**
All rights reserved. No part of this publication may be
reproduced, stored in a retrieval system or be transmitted in
any form or by any means, electronic, mechanical, photocopying,
recording, or otherwise, without the prior written permission
of Crabtree Publishing Company. In Canada: We acknowledge the
financial support of the Government of Canada through the Book
Publishing Industry Development Program (BPIDP) for our
publishing activities.

Cataloging-in-Publication Data
MacAulay, Kelley.
  Goldfish / Kelley MacAulay & Bobbie Kalman ; illustrations by
Margaret Amy Reiach ; photographs by Marc Crabtree.
      p. cm. -- (Pet care series)
  Includes index.
  ISBN 0-7787-1759-3 (RLB) -- ISBN 0-7787-1791-7 (pbk.)
  1. Goldfish--Juvenile literature. I. Kalman, Bobbie. II. Reiach,
Margaret Amy, ill. III. Crabtree, Marc, ill. IV. Title. V. Series.
  SF458.G6M33 2004
  639.3'7484--dc22
                                                    2004011116
                                                          LC

**Published in
the United States**
PMB16A
350 Fifth Ave.
Suite 3308
New York, NY
10118

**Published
in Canada**
616 Welland Ave.,
St. Catharines, Ontario,
Canada
L2M 5V6

**Published in the
United Kingdom**
73 Lime Walk
Headington
Oxford
OX3 7AD
United Kingdom

**Published
in Australia**
386 Mt. Alexander Rd.,
Ascot Vale (Melbourne)
VIC 3032

Contents

What are goldfish?

Goldfish are a type of **fish**. Fish are animals that live in water. They use **gills** to breathe. All fish have two gills. Fish use their **fins** and tails to move through water. The body of a fish is protected by **scales**.

A goldfish's body

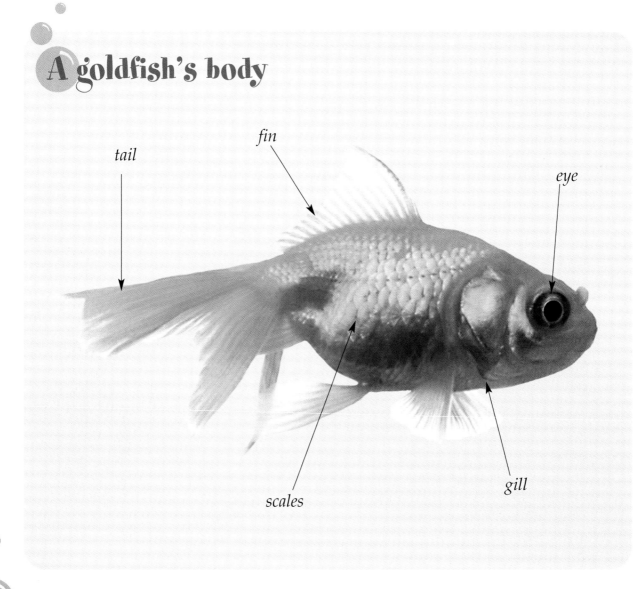

tail

fin

eye

scales

gill

Close relatives

Pet goldfish are related to **wild fish** called crucian carps. Wild fish are not kept as pets. Goldfish are similar to crucian carps, except for their colors and the shapes of their fins. Crucian carps are brown and gray, whereas goldfish are orange and gold. Crucian carps have rounded fins, whereas goldfish fins are pointed.

The first people to keep goldfish as pets lived in China over 1,000 years ago. Today, goldfish are among the most popular pets in the world.

The right pet for you?

It is fun to watch a bright, colorful goldfish swim around a fish tank. Keeping a goldfish healthy is a lot of work, however. You will have to feed your goldfish every day. The fish tank also needs to be cleaned every week. An adult will have to help you with these important jobs.

Would you take good care of a goldfish?

Are you ready?

The questions below will help you and your family decide if you are ready for a goldfish.

🐟 Fish tanks can be expensive. Is your family prepared to buy a good tank for your goldfish?

🐟 Some fish tanks are quite large. Do you have room in your home for a fish tank?

🐟 Will you feed your goldfish every day?

🐟 Will someone help you clean the fish tank at least once a week?

🐟 Do you have other pets that may try to scare or harm your goldfish?

Goldfish breeds

There are over 100 **breeds**, or kinds, of goldfish! All the breeds belong to one of two types of goldfish. The two types of goldfish are **ordinary goldfish** and **fancy goldfish**. Ordinary goldfish have only one tail, whereas fancy goldfish have two tails. These pages show some popular goldfish breeds.

The common goldfish is an ordinary goldfish. It has a slim body, which makes this fish a good swimmer.

Another ordinary goldfish is the
shubunkin. It has unusual colorings.
The shubunkin is light blue with
orange and black markings.

The oranda is one of
the most popular fancy
goldfish breeds. Like
many fancy goldfish, the
oranda has a round body.

The bubble-eye goldfish is a
fancy goldfish. This breed has
a large bubble under each eye.

Baby goldfish

Baby goldfish are called **fry**. Fry **hatch** from eggs laid by their mothers. Adult goldfish eat the eggs, so the parents must be moved to a different fish tank after the mother has laid her eggs. The fry hatch from the eggs in three to seven days.

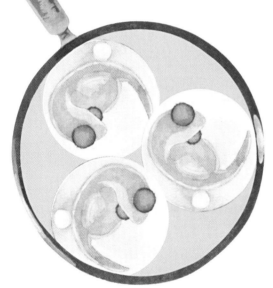

When you look at a goldfish egg upclose, you can see a tiny goldfish growing inside.

Goldfish eggs are small and sticky. They attach to the plastic plants in the fish tank.

Outside the eggs

After hatching, the fry do not move for at least two days. During this time, they eat the food that is left in their eggs. As soon as they begin to swim, the fry start searching for food. They need to eat special food three times a day.

It takes two months before fry begin to look like adult goldfish.

No unwanted goldfish!

You do not have to worry that your goldfish will lay eggs. Goldfish **mate** only in water that is colder than the water in your fish tank. If you want your goldfish to mate, remember that it is difficult to care for fry. Make sure you can take care of all the babies or find them good homes.

Getting ready

Before you bring your goldfish home, get everything ready for your new pet. Some of the things that you will need to care for your goldfish properly are shown on these pages.

Choose a large glass fish tank.

A sticker **thermometer** allows you to check the water temperature in the tank every day.

A **filter** helps keep the water in your fish tank clean.

Buy some packaged food to feed your goldfish.

Place your fish tank on a strong stand.

You will also need a metal thermometer to use while cleaning your fish tank.

Special drops keep the water in your fish tank healthy for your goldfish.

Your tank should have a **hood**, or cover.

You will need a small net to scoop old food out of the tank.

Your fish tank needs a light. Choose one with a **fluorescent** bulb. Fluorescent bulbs will not heat the water in your fish tank.

A **gravel vacuum** will help you clean your fish tank.

Adding a paper background to the back of your fish tank will make it more colorful.

Cover the bottom of your fish tank with **gravel**.

Toys will make your fish tank look more interesting.

Plastic plants give your goldfish places to hide!

The fish tank

You can buy a fish tank at a pet store. Goldfish need to live in a lot of water to be healthy. Choose a long fish tank made of glass. Two large goldfish need a fish tank that holds at least ten gallons (38 liters) of water. Keep in mind that your goldfish may not be fully grown when you buy them!

Goldfish should never live in a small fish bowl.

The perfect place

Before setting up your fish tank, you need to choose the perfect place for it in your home. Do not place the fish tank near a window. Sunlight shining on the tank will heat the water and make your goldfish sick. It is also important to put your fish tank on a strong stand. A fish tank filled with water is very heavy!

Setting up the fish tank

Once you have chosen the right place for your fish tank, you can begin setting it up. First, wash the tank, the filter, and the plastic plants with a mixture of water and salt. Next, place the gravel in a bucket and wash it with plenty of water. Do not use soap to clean anything that will be in your fish tank. Soap makes goldfish sick.

Almost ready

Once the fish tank is set up, fill it with water and add the special drops. The water temperature should be between 60°F (16°C) and 70°F (21°C). Set up your fish tank a few days before you bring your goldfish home. Setting up the tank early will allow you to make sure the water is just right for your goldfish.

toy

paper background   hood   thermometer

plastic plant   gravel

Choosing your goldfish

You can get goldfish from a pet store or from a **breeder**. You can also ask your friends and family if they know of anyone who is giving goldfish away. Make sure you pick a goldfish that is living in very clean water. A goldfish likes living with other goldfish. If you buy more than one goldfish, make sure all the fish are the same breed. Some goldfish cost less than other goldfish do. Cheaper goldfish are not as healthy as more expensive goldfish, however.

When choosing your goldfish, keep in mind that it is easier to care for an ordinary goldfish than it is to care for a fancy goldfish.

What to look for

Take your time picking the goldfish you want as your pet. You can tell if a goldfish is healthy if:

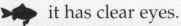 it has clear eyes.

 the fins do not droop and are not torn.

it has no missing scales.

there are no bumps on the goldfish.

 it is a strong swimmer.

Into the tank!

You will bring your goldfish home from the pet store in a plastic bag. Do not put your goldfish directly into the tank, however! Your goldfish need time to get used to the water temperature in your fish tank. Follow the steps on these pages to help your goldfish adjust to their new home.

Place the unopened bag that holds your goldfish into the fish tank and let it float for fifteen minutes.

After fifteen minutes, open the plastic bag and add some water from the fish tank to the bag. Then close the bag and let it float for another fifteen minutes.

Finally, open the bag and allow your goldfish to swim out into the fish tank.

Goldfish food

Goldfish love to eat! They will eat as much food as you give them, even if it makes them sick. Feed your goldfish twice a day. Your goldfish should be able to finish eating their meal in about five minutes. If your goldfish take longer than five minutes to eat, give them less food the next time you feed them.

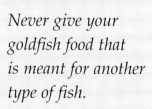

Never give your goldfish food that is meant for another type of fish.

Different foods

Goldfish need to eat a variety of foods to be healthy. Buy packaged food for your goldfish at a pet store. Packaged food comes as flakes or pellets. Your goldfish should also be fed frozen goldfish food, such as shrimp. Once a week you can feed your goldfish **raw**, or uncooked, shrimp as a treat. Make sure the shrimp has been carefully washed before you give it to the goldfish.

Daily goldfish care

Goldfish are easier to care for than some other pets because you do not need to walk them or play with them! However, there are some jobs you need to do every day to make sure your goldfish stay healthy.

Check the sticker thermometer daily to make sure the water temperature in your fish tank is between 60°F (16°C) to 70°F (21°C).

Before feeding your goldfish, use a small net to remove old food from the fish tank.

Check to make sure the filter is working properly.

Your goldfish will go to sleep at night when your house is dark. To help your fish get a good night's rest, turn off the light in the fish tank.

Cleaning the fish tank

You will need an adult to help you clean your fish tank. Cleaning a fish tank is a big job! You can make it easier by doing a little cleaning every week. The most important job is removing some of the water from the tank each week to add fresh water.

algae scraper

Before changing the water in the tank, have an adult use an algae scraper to clean the inside walls of the tank.

Fresh water

Clean your fish tank with a gravel vacuum.
The vacuum cleans the tank by sucking
dirt and old food out of the gravel. The
gravel vacuum also removes some water
from the tank. Stop the vacuum when
one-quarter of the water has been removed.
Next, add some fresh water to the tank.
Before you add the water, use the metal
thermometer to make sure the fresh water
is the same temperature as the water in
the tank.

Staying safe

Your goldfish will be safe inside a clean fish tank, but there are still some things you can do to make sure it does not get scared or hurt. These pages show what you can do to protect your goldfish.

Other pets, such as cats, can seriously injure your goldfish.

*Knocking on the
fish tank will scare
your goldfish.*

Goldfish like living with other
fish, but some types of fish, such
as the angelfish above, will harm
goldfish. Before adding new fish to
your fish tank, ask someone at a pet
store which types of fish get along
well with goldfish.

*Remember that your fish tank is
made of breakable glass. Never play
games near your fish tank that
may cause you to break the tank.*

Healthy goldfish

A **veterinarian** or "vet" is a medical doctor who treats animals. He or she will help you keep your goldfish healthy. If you think your goldfish may be sick, contact your vet or someone at your pet store right away. The sooner your goldfish is treated for the illness, the better its chances are of staying alive!

If you notice one of your goldfish showing signs of illness, separate it from the other goldfish in the tank right away. Put the sick goldfish into another tank.

When to get help

It is very important to take your goldfish to a vet at the first sign of an illness. Watch for any of the warning signs listed below.

- Check for bumps or tiny bugs on the body of your goldfish.

- A sick goldfish may breathe rapidly.

- Make sure there are no white spots on the body of your goldfish.

- Watch for missing parts on the tail or fins.

Best friends

You must spend time caring for your goldfish every day. You need to feed it and to make sure it has a clean place to live. Happy, healthy goldfish can live for ten years. Enjoy your goldfish!

Words to know

Note: Boldfaced words that are defined in the book may not appear in the glossary.

algae scraper A tool used to scrape off tiny green plants that grow on the sides of fish tanks

breeder A person who brings goldfish together so the fish can make babies

gill The part of a fish that is used for breathing

hatch To break out of an egg

mate To join together to make babies

scale One of many thin, hard plates that cover the body of a goldfish

thermometer A tool that measures the water temperature in a fish tank

Index

1 2 3 4 5 6 7 8 9 0 Printed in the U.S.A. 4 3 2 1 0 9 8 7 6 5